MINING

Nicolas Brasch

Rigby

www.Rigby.com
1-800-531-5015

Rigby Focus Forward

Published in 2007 by Nelson Australia Pty Ltd ACN: 058 280 149
A Cengage Learning company

1 2 3 4 5 6 7 8 374 14 13 12 11 10 09 08 07
Printed and bound in China

Mining
ISBN-13   978-1-4190-3827-3
ISBN-10   1-4190-3827-3

Acknowledgments
The author and publisher would like to acknowledge permission to reproduce material from the following sources:
Photographs by AAP Image/AFP Photo/Pool, p. 20; Auscape/ Terry Whittaker, p. 21; Fotolia/ Graca Victoria, p. 9 bottom/ Mark Smith, p. 10/ Paul Moore, back cover top, p. 5/ Stuart Monk, pp. 8-9 bottom; Getty Images/ Paul Chesley, p. 23 right/ Stockbyte Platinum, p. 17/ Taxi, p. 15/ The Image Bank, back cover bottom, 3, 6, 12 bottom, 22 left; Harcourt Telescope/ Corel royalty-free p. 19; Istockphoto, p. 8 top, 22 right/ Achim Prill, p. 8 bottom/ Craig Hill, p. 13 bottom/ Frances Wicks, p. 13 top/ Jeffrey Sheldon, p. 9 top/ Zsolt Biczó, p. 11 left; Photolibrary/ Neil Duncan, front cover, pp. 1, 4, 7/ Pierre Cheuva/Photononstop, p. 18/ Robin Smith, p. 14/ SPL/ Robert Brook, p. 16/ SPL/ Pascal Goetgheluck, pp. 8-9 top/ SPL/ US Dept of Energy, p. 12 top/ WK Fletcher, p. 23 left.

MINING

Nicolas Brasch

Contents

Chapter 1

MINING

Mining involves digging up **minerals** and other **natural resources** from under the earth's surface. These minerals and natural resources are used for a variety of reasons.

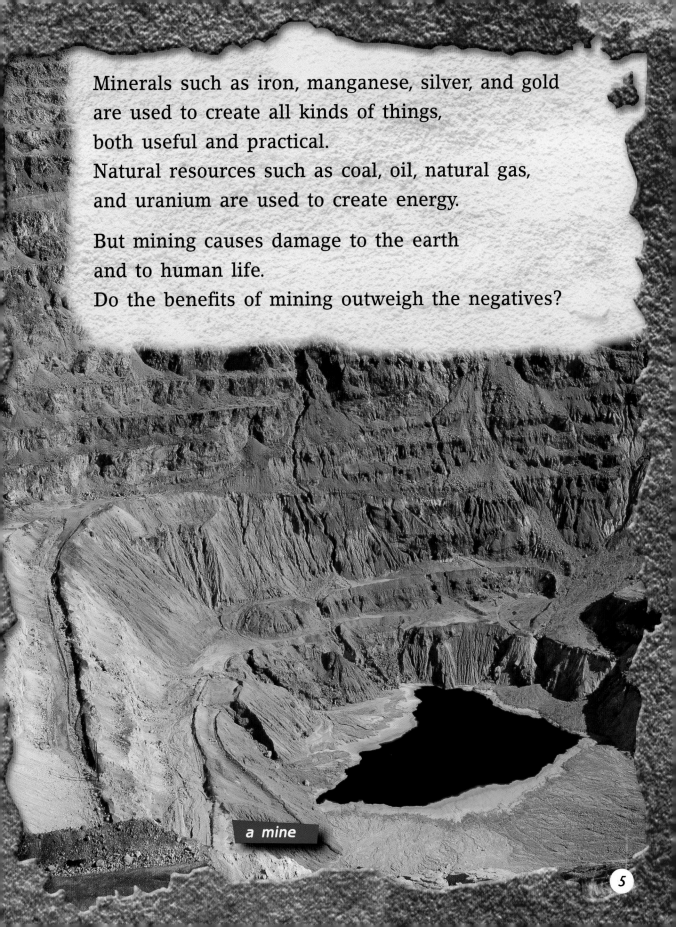

Minerals such as iron, manganese, silver, and gold
are used to create all kinds of things,
both useful and practical.
Natural resources such as coal, oil, natural gas,
and uranium are used to create energy.

But mining causes damage to the earth
and to human life.
Do the benefits of mining outweigh the negatives?

a mine

Chapter 2

THE PROS OF MINING

Economic Value

Mining is a huge industry.

It is worth billions of dollars around the world.

If all mining was stopped tomorrow,

most **economies** around the world would suffer.

There would be high unemployment,

and many people would run out of money.

a gold mine in Papua New Guinea

Mining provides income for people living in
developing countries that have minerals
and natural resources.
People in these developing countries can then
feed, house, and educate themselves.

Examples of these developing countries are
Papua New Guinea, Jamaica,
Suriname, Guinea, and Bolivia.

What Minerals Are Used For

Many minerals discovered in the ground are used to create things that are used all around us.

jewelry

knives and forks

pots

coins

talcum powder

Producing Energy

One of the most important uses
of the earth's natural resources
is as a source of energy.
Coal, oil, natural gas, and uranium
are natural resources that are mined
and used to create energy.

coal

Coal is used to produce electricity,
which **illuminates** homes and offices
and powers equipment.

gasoline

natural gas

Oil is used to produce gasoline,
which powers cars and other forms of transportation.

Natural gas is used to produce heat.

Uranium is used to create **nuclear energy,**
which is used to make electricity.
Using nuclear energy to create electricity
is more efficient than using coal.

The energy created by 1.3 million pounds of coal
makes about the same amount of energy
as using one pound of uranium.

uranium

a nuclear power plant

a hydroelectric power plant

a wind power farm

If coal, oil, natural gas, and uranium were not mined, people would have to find alternative energy sources, which may be more costly and less efficient to use.

Chapter 3

THE CONS OF MINING

Environmental Damage

Mining the earth has several environmental consequences:

- The earth's landscape is destroyed by mining equipment.

- Animal and plant habitats are destroyed, which can lead to the extinction of animal and plant species.

• Waste materials from mines can pollute streams and other water sources.

- The landscape becomes an **eyesore**.

- Valuable natural resources are used up.

But if people invested in renewable
natural energy sources today,
such as wind and the sun,
they would be helping future generations.
While the earth's natural resources are limited
and will eventually disappear,
many people think that investing in
renewable energy sources
is much too costly to consider.

Indigenous Land Rights

In some continents, like North America,
South America, and Australia,
land that is mined has significant religious, spiritual,
and cultural value to indigenous people.

A new mine provides income for a mining company.
But to indigenous people, a new mine
often means the destruction of the land they value.
Some mining companies are sympathetic
to the religious, spiritual, and cultural values
of indigenous people,
but other mining companies ignore them.

Safety Concerns

Mining is a very dangerous industry.
Thousands of miners around the world
are killed every year at work.
They can be killed because of underground explosions,
mines caving in, and broken equipment.

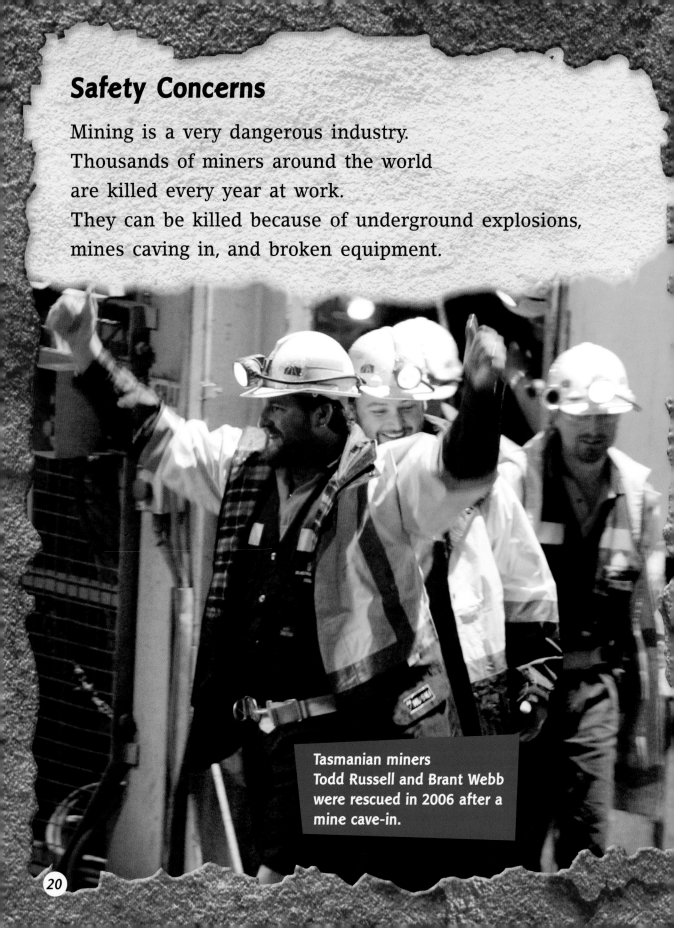

Tasmanian miners
Todd Russell and Brant Webb
were rescued in 2006 after a
mine cave-in.

a polluted water supply

Despite tight safety controls, there is also a risk
to miners mining some dangerous materials like uranium.

But mining is not only dangerous to the people who work
in the mining industry.
It can also be dangerous for the public.
Water that has been polluted by the mining process
can find its way into public water supplies.

CONCLUSION

Mining Pros

- Many people depend on mining to support their families.

- Many countries depend on income from mining.

- Minerals are used to make the things around us such as kitchen utensils, coins, and even talcum powder.

- Mined resources such as coal, oil, natural gas, and uranium are used to create energy.

Mining Cons

- The earth's landscape is destroyed by the mining process.

- Animal and plant species' habitats can be lost, and species can become extinct.

- Mining can cause important natural resources to be used up.

- Mining can ruin land that has religious, spiritual, or cultural value to indigenous people.

- Mining can be very dangerous for those that work in the industry.

Glossary

economies   a country's activities relating to the production, distribution, exchange, and consumption of goods and services

eyesore   something that is ugly to look at

illuminates   lights up

minerals   natural compounds formed by geological processes

natural resources   naturally occurring substances considered valuable

nuclear energy   energy created by a controlled nuclear reaction

Index